JUST FOR YOU TODAY

Norman Fearon

MINERVA PRESS
LONDON
ATLANTA MONTREUX SYDNEY

JUST FOR YOU TODAY
Copyright © Norman Fearon 1998

All Rights Reserved

No part of this book may be reproduced in any form,
by photocopying or by any electronic or mechanical means,
including information storage or retrieval systems,
without permission in writing from both the copyright
owner and the publisher of this book.

ISBN 0 75410 068 5

First Published 1998 by
MINERVA PRESS
Sixth Floor
Canberra House
315–317 Regent Street
London W1R 7YB

2nd Impression 1998

Printed in Great Britain for Minerva Press

JUST FOR YOU TODAY

Endeavour to read the Scripture passage relevant to the text, either Authorised Version or New International Version.

Christian Greetings Book

Ideal for birthdays, anniversaries, celebrations, festivals, Christmas and New Year.

Short reflections, covering sixty-one days, offering help and inspiration to all who read them.

The author is a long-serving reader in the Church, a retired pharmacist and member of the Royal Pharmaceutical Society.

To
....

With best wishes from

....

Day One

> I have learnt to be content, whatever the circumstances, I know what it is to be in need, and I know what it is to have plenty...
>
> Philippians 4:11–12

There is a lot of truth in the old saying, 'A faint heart ne'er won a fair lady'. One of the best things we can do for this world is to show it ever a victorious life of joy, a face that that shines even through the tears, a beauty of the Lord which glows with pure radiance. A little verse runs:

> Joys that cost nothing give us little pleasure,
> We value most, the things most hardly won,
> Men that delve deep to find earth's hidden treasure,
> Would pass it by, if open to the sun.

The apostle, St Paul, was wearing a heavy chain in prison when he wrote, 'I have learnt to be content'. He had to learn – it wasn't always so – he had to go to school, to chafe amid his prison discomforts, to find he couldn't have all his own way, all the time. It did not come easily, any more than it does for you and I to have peace in our hearts and chains on our hands or legs. neither did this ideal way of living come all at once, immediately he embraced the Christian way. He had to reach out to it through the power of the

Holy Spirit of God; by prayer, by reading, by struggle, by discipline, by experiences of life, grave and gay.

A good pianist must practise the scales: mastering the multiplication tables is the secret to good arithmetic. An artist painted life as a dark, storm-swept sea, covered with wrecks. He also painted, in the midst of wild waves, a great rock, in a cleft of which, high up amid herbage and flowers, was a dove sitting quietly on her nest. Peace even with chaos all around, contentment. On the rock of our Lord Jesus Christ, being in the cleft of His love and care is the true mark of contentment, it makes all the difference.

Day Two

All the rivers run into the sea, yet the sea is not full...

Ecclesiastes 1:7

Here is a most engaging sentence, full of unfathomable depth, showing the wonder, might and wisdom of the Creator. Rivers in flood and seas that overflow bring catastrophe and problems far beyond the human mind.

Life itself is a mystery only enlightened in God. The hymn writer says, 'Change and decay in all around I see... O Thou, who changest not, abide with me.' Time is short and man's work is never done, like the sea ebbing and flowing, with waves rolling to and fro, and side to side. Man, the restless creature, is never satisfied, never content. The more the world offers, the more men would have; we find the good life yet we remain unsatisfied and disillusioned. the ocean, despite all the rivers that run into it, is still a troubled sea that cannot rest; it is not yet full. The more we receive in this life, humanly speaking, the more peevish we may become, crying, 'Give me, give me, give me – wealth, health, longer life, better conditions, security, pleasure, children and so on.'

The great mystery of God requires our whole intellect and still leaves us baffled, above all, it requires our hearts and experience. There must a response with penitence, faith, obedience and love. Are our inner depths stirred and moved? Is there a new depth of life? St Paul writes, 'I no longer live, but Christ lives in me.' Meaning, we are a new creature in Christ in a real and deep sense, with His thoughts, outlook, sympathies and ideals. His will and purpose enter into our being to bring us His joy and peace. With prayer, Bible reading, worship and Communion, the inner and secret means combine with the ordinary outward means to enable us to live well towards others and God, and the wonders of nature cause us to marvel and glorify Him.

> In heavenly love abiding,
> No change my heart shall fear;
> And safe in such abiding,
> For nothing changes here.

Anna L. Waring
1850

Day Three

They shall ask the way to Zion with their faces thitherward...

Jeremiah 50:5

Immediately after Christ's discourse on divorce, the Bible tells about some parents who were concerned for the good of their children. They brought them to Jesus, who defends the family, womanhood and children. However, the disciples rebuked these parents and discouraged them. They endeavoured to send them away. Jesus was displeased with these misguided actions and spoke those lovely words which are the children's charter: 'Suffer the little children to come unto Me, and forbid them not for of such is the Kingdom of God.' (St Mark 10:13–16). Notice the word 'little', none are too small or too young, do not despise this action. They weren't ill, they were brought so that He might touch them, but Jesus did a great deal more – He always does – It has been said: He had no children that He might adopt all children. this includes young people as well. Jesus found Philip and he became a disciple. Philip told Nathaniel and he came. Andrew told Peter and he came and so on, Christianity being built on the words and actions of these young men, touched by Christ (St John 1:40–50).

The works of our Lord Jesus Christ are creative and beneficent. It is He alone who can give the blessings we all need. Character, new life, the best begins with Jesus as we place our trust and faith in His redeeming love, and go through life in His care.

> The Lord's my shepherd, I'll not want:
> He makes me down to lie
> In pastures green; He leadeth me
> The quiet waters by.

Francis Rous
1579

Day Four

Almost you persuade me to be a Christian.

Acts 26:28

Only three times does the word Christian appear in the Bible. The Christian religion means a great deal and claims to give us a faith, a hope and a love, which can survive all the chances and changes of this mortal life. The Gospel lays the ghosts of the 'human' life and sets before us the promises and blessings of the 'Eternal' life. The Apostle, St Paul, in Acts 26 spoke of this and the amazing changes in his own personal life brought about by the life, death and Resurrection of our Lord Jesus Christ, when speaking before King Agrippa and his retinue. So much so, that the king was moved almost to be persuaded to embrace the Christian faith but sad to say, failed to pursue his convictions. Acts 11:26 tells us that 'the disciples were called Christians first at Antioch.' This means that for all time, followers now put their dependence upon Jesus who is the Christ. We must do nothing to reproach the worthy name and devote ourselves entirely to the sacred honour of the One whose name we bear.

Again, in 1 Peter 4:16, we read, 'If you suffer as a Christian, do not be ashamed, but praise God that you bear that name.' This means it is an honour to be included in the community of people called Christians, living a life of newness and power of the Holy Spirit despite what it may cost to do so.

Even in the Christian religion there are rivalries between this Church and that, between ministers and members, services and meetings. People become jealous and easily take offence. It may mean that some get the work, while other get the credit, ordinary folk filling the breach and perhaps not filling it too well or easily. Suffering can bring out the best in us. The early Christians went about as witnesses to the faith in our Lord Jesus Christ convincing men and women in an electrifying manner that they had been with Jesus. The credibility of such people was so obviously honest, because in them was produced, through Christ, a different kind of life, showing forth the fruit of the Spirit, (Galatians 5:22). Then others are persuaded to become Christians and to praise God.

A little tot was asked, 'How old are you?' He answered, 'I'se not old, I'se new.' Remember that you are new, don't fall away, make a good start on Christ's way; that leads to a life that is life indeed.

Day Five

[Jesus said,] 'The poor you will always have with you, but you will not always have me.'

St Matthew 26:11

Life often brings tragedy difficult to understand. Take child abuse brought on in dire poverty. The parents have no job, no likely prospects of achieving employment, no money, no help, no friends, little possessions, clothes, furniture or comforts. Destitute people, victims of disaster, with tragic little ones deprived of parental love, facing days of utter bleakness. Some children are born disabled; the required special care overwhelms the mother and she seeks another life elsewhere. Often it is the father who leaves and terrific debts remain behind to be faced. Drink and sex are often precursors of such situations. Many divorces leave behind strange and devastating realities, particularly for young children and the not so young. tragic loss and violence have acquired a high profile in our time, and are incredibly common. The emergency departments of the hospitals support this fact, with numerous injuries caused by domestic strife, many life-threatening. Often they are said to be inflicted by undefined causes: 'hit by a lead pipe', 'fell in the kitchen', 'banged her head' – passive phrases hiding savage acts. Release from hospital can mean a return in fear to the same problems, with the threat of reprisal together with an inability to support themselves or their family without a partner. A truly wretched picture made worse by the so-called drug scene: the attempt to cushion people from the unpleasant realities of life and to induce feelings of euphoria and superiority. As long as money and fortunes can be made, the illicit traffic in drugs will remain, despite the sheltered lives of many in our society. All around are pirates ready to take over lives.

The touchstone for you and me is simply this: our passion for God and the Lord Jesus Christ, our personal love for Him. Whether ways of life be right or wrong, we can be very, very clear; if they take the fine edge off your devotion, public or private, for the Master; if they cause the flame in your heart to flicker out or lessen in the slightest degree, your vision of the Saviour on the Cross, then you need to pray and seek what you need to do to aid those who badly require help.

Day Six

You must be born again. The wind blows wherever it pleases. You hear the sound, but you cannot tell where it comes from or where it is going, so it is with everyone born of the spirit. 'How can this be?' Nicodemus asked.

St John 3:7–9

There is a well-known street in Grimsby called Garibaldi Street. Who was this person? In the dark days of struggle for liberty in Italy, Garibaldi was regarded as the great liberator. Prisoners being hurried away to terrible dungeons were encouraged on their way along the streets by people whispering, 'Garibaldi is coming, take courage.' Men would steal out at night and write on the walls and pavements, 'Garibaldi is coming'. As he approached the city, they found freedom, never to be slaves again.

One far greater has come, the great deliverer from slavery and sin, bringing redemption and freedom. He is Jesus Christ, our Lord.

In the New Testament, Nicodemus, a Pharisee, ruler of the Jews and a good man, had heard of Jesus, heard of His teaching and maybe knew of His parables and miracles, yet other leaders and Pharisees hated Jesus. Nicodemus was puzzled, he sought out Christ, coming secretly by night; he was shy and timid, despite being a man of authority, brainy, wealthy, well educated with everything going for him. He approached his enquiries with care, warily. He congratulated Jesus, who, though probably tired, found time for him. Jesus always has time for men and women. He answered his questions and spoke to him about a new birth. 'Ye must be born again.' This is a spiritual rebirth, born from above by the power of the Holy Spirit, who carries forward in the world the work and influence of God.

We all can now have access to Jesus. Once a limited few were touched and healed and helped. Some even had to fight their way to Him. Blind Bartimaeus shouted, Zaccheus climbed into a tree, a shy woman touched the hem of His garment, four friends let another man down through an open roof. Some in great need missed Him altogether, yet Jesus included all in His scope. Now unfettered, His Spirit continues His saving grace and 'He is coming again'. 'Whoever believes in Him shall not perish but have Eternal Life.'

> I cannot tell why He, whom angels worship,
> Should set his love upon the sons of men,
> Or why, as Shepherd, He should seek the wanderers
> To bring them back, they know not how or when.

> W.Y. Fullerton
> 1929

Day Seven

> Rend your heart and not your garments, and turn unto the Lord your God: for he is gracious and merciful, slow to anger and of great kindness...
>
> Joel 2:13

Notable today are extreme agitators who attempt to pressurise folk with activities they claim to be beneficial so that others will opt out and leave them in control. Benefits used to bribe and induce power are sometimes incapable of being honoured as were the empty charades of Satan in the temptation of our Lord Jesus Christ. The prophet Joel speaks of a plague of locusts, a dreaded experience and invasion characteristic of the East. Overwhelming numbers of the locusts darken the sky, the air is crowded, the plants devoured. The houses are infested leaving famine and disease, with people and beasts in despair.

The vision of the prophet is of the judgement of God, the wrath of the Creator upon the unrepentant, the blessing of God on those who turn to Him. This illustrates the great contrast between good and evil, truth and falsehood; between a God-fearing and loving people and those who refuse God and His ways. There is a judgement coming of those who fear God and work righteousness and those who do the reverse.

I will pour out my spirit upon all flesh, whosoever shall call upon the name of the Lord, shall be saved.

Acts 2:17

In Jesus we can perceive the Spirit of God. The Father and His Son, perfect Man, to take upon Himself our human flesh. Born of His Mother into this world, suffering for our salvation, now ascended into Heaven, perfect God, from whence He shall judge the living and the dead, giving account of their own works.

It is important to guard against anything that takes inordinate, unwanted possession of our lives, and to affirm our beliefs and faith.

An Arab was with his camel, the night was cold, the camel sought permission to put his nose inside his master's tent. A few minutes later, his head followed, soon his front legs were in and before long, the camel, hump and all, were filling the whole tent. It was in possession. A lesson plain to see.

Day Eight

> And Sarah said, 'God hath made me to laugh, so that all that hear will laugh with me.'
>
> Genesis 21:6

Despite today's stupendous scientific advances, we are burdened with untold stress and strain. People are not happy in the true sense; frustration, stress, anxiety and abandonment meet us daily, wherever we are – through those with whom we have contact, in the papers we read, the radio we hear, the television we see. Young folk are wanting to turn to someone, and seek somewhere for an outlet for all the bottled-up feeling inside. They turn to 'pop', to scream, scream and scream. Yeah, yeah, yeah!

In one of the major cities, the Samaritans receive over one thousand calls annually dealing with desperate cases; people on the verge of suicide, men and women seeking help, trying to find someone to turn to in their worries.

A change is good from a life centred in self and in things, to one centred in God. We find a sense of new direction and values. Not what do *I* want in or from life, not what does the world, my friends family and associates want or say about life, but what does *God* say or want from me and my life. It isn't an opiate for living or escapism, it is being involved and committed, ceasing to be a spectator, beginning to be a partaker. What can *I* do to help others to look and turn to God, the author and giver of life.

I love a good laugh, I love to see people laughing with me, it is one of the great gifts of God, wonderful! Why did Sarah laugh? Because, contrary to nature and all its laws, she, in old age, gave birth to a son. She saw in Isaac God's gift and laughed in rapture and joy, and all her friends laughed with her.

When the Holy Spirit of God dwells within us, in our dry, withered barren, sin-ridden lives, and we find the Lord Jesus Christ has changed us, our desert blooms and blossoms with fruit unto holiness. His grace and companionship are ours for ever. I rejoice in this salvation. I surprise my family with my new life, I delight my friends with my ever-increasing joy. I impress the world with my ways and conversation. Jesus is my unspeakable joy. 'He has made me to laugh so that all that hear will laugh with me.'

Day Nine

...that He may do His work, His strange work; and bring to pass His act, His strange act.

Isaiah 28:21

It is not unknown that certain people are tempted to believe in God as a comprehensive insurance policy against the future, just in case, there is an afterlife with the alternative of Heaven or Hell.

All will be well, Heaven is covered and sure, even on 'New for Old' terms. Or they may try to treat belief as if there was an advance ticket, booking a place as for a continental holiday in some pleasant away place with luxurious accommodation, excellent food, magnificent surroundings, warm sunny weather and lovely friendly people. Pie in the sky, it is called. Belief and faith in God have nothing to do with human trust such as that. Chapter 4 in the Book of Daniel gives the story of King Nebuchadnezzar. After thirty-five years of reign he dreamed of a great tree being cut down to the stump and seeks the prophet, Daniel, to interpret the dream. It is a message of judgement. The king was overcome by pride, the awful thing that transforms men and women, believing they are way above others. Here is Nebuchadnezzar, a mighty soldier, and a king destroying cities and men, but also building walls, palaces, temples and nations.

He is mindful of his own power, greatness and glory. Pride makes us self-reliant – my gifts, my achievements, my qualities. Beware of pride, it is a cheat and a liar. So the king became 'cut down', stark mad, living with the beasts of the fields, eating grass wet with dew, nails like claws with a disease called today, lycanthropy; animal in nature. Sanity and emotional health are closely linked to giving God His rightful place. After seven years, the King's madness leaves him, he is again in his right mind, once more mighty and praising God. But he has learnt three things – God's rule is eternal, His power is unequalled, (we can work with Him or without Him, the choice is ours), and God is responsible to no other. We live between the tangible world of today and the unfathomable world of the future when the whole truth of history will be revealed as accomplishing the purposes of God.

Day Ten

> You have been weighed on the balances and found wanting... That very night, Belshazzar... was slain and Darius took over the Kingdom.
>
> Daniel 5:27–31

Today we live in stirring times. News worldwide travels almost instantaneously; momentous events take place, not always for the good and best, sometimes in our own lives and families.

Democracy is the great theme in a very materialistic world, with a clamour for social harmony and economic justice. Quite often people concede to despots and families and societies fall apart. Fallen human nature and the flawed inner lives of men and women cause nations and peoples to collapse. Standing at the cross-roads, we see pointers to worldwide global or nuclear wars, financial intractable problems, erosions of nations, together with the call of God for His Kingdom, through His faithful messengers. it is never to late to change direction. 'The writing is on the wall', is one of the best-known narrations in the Bible. A story of a gay king becoming a gloomy wretch, in fear at the feast, Belshazzar had devastated Jerusalem and later been driven back to Babylon by the Medes, hopelessly routed.

They were now under siege in Babylon but it was a very secure place, the River Euphrates was its bulwark; they had many years provisions. Even so, it was not time for a riotous, idolatrous and sacrilegious feast, rather it was time for a fast. When the writing appeared on the wall, they could neither read nor interpret it. His guilty conscience told him that the end was in sight, his life was at stake. The impregnable heights were scaled by the enemy, they were inside the city and that very night Belshazzar was slain.

Self-destructive irreligious ways bring insoluble problems. The answer is to follow the prophet Daniel and stay close to God who rules the hearts and destiny of us all. Jesus whispers to his followers 'Lo, I am with you always, even to the end.'

Day Eleven

...as long as he sought the Lord, God made him to prosper... when he was strong, his heart was lifted up to his destruction...

2 Chronicles 26:5–16

King Uzziah was flooded with success, became proud and strong in self-confidence. The heart of a man proved too much, beaten by self.

> Oh, why should the spirit of mortal be proud?
> Like a fast falling meteor and a fast flying cloud,
> A flash of lightening and break of the wave,
> He passes from life to rest in the grave.

Mortality by William Knox

The king's father was killed by mob violence and popular choice determined his son Uzziah be king. He was only sixteen years old, a difficult age, yet his was a long reign of fifty-two years. He sought God, the finest thing he could do. He battled against the enemy, the Philistines, and 'God helped him'. When we fight against evil people and evil ways God will help us: as in sport, the team take the offensive and take heart, the supporters cheer and roar with joy. Uzziah built protective towers and fortified Jerusalem.

He increased agriculture and husbandry, he ordered wells to be dug in the dry and thirsty land. What of our battling and building day by day? Sadly, Uzziah desired not only the kingship but the priestly office, expressly forbidden by law. He entered the Temple, committed sacrilege and soon ended in an unkingly grave. In a dramatic scene, he became a leper, a malignant affliction in his head. Separated from his throne and people, his was a living death, beaten to a bitter end.

As we stop to take spiritual stock, to make up the account, the things that really matter; how are we doing, is it gain or loss? Do we stand well, where we are placed; boldly and fearlessly for God and Christ and righteousness, at home, at work, school and on the highways of life, or has there been a sad falling away?

Day Twelve

In the year that King Uzziah died, I saw also the Lord...

Isaiah 6:1

Two men looked through prison bars, one saw mud, the other stars. All-important in life is vision. The past is all very well, the present may be good, bad or indifferent. The future always holds out the promise – of what? Of better things to come. Hope springs eternal in the human breast.

Isaiah received the news of the sad end of King Uzziah; he also was to receive a vision of God for his own life and ways. Only the Creator can transform us and our situations in life, He can turn us upside down and inside out. The king was dead, the prophet was moved, hopes were shattered, the future looked bleak. There was the threat of war, fears and forbodings, anxieties and a sense of loss; underneath was a national, deep, moral and spiritual decay. Cast utterly back on God, Isaiah sought the quiet of the Temple. We can picture him slowly climbing the steps, in a pensive mood, entering with sad and solemn steps. Yet a little while he comes out with springing feet and lightened heart. Now what is the great secret, the lesson for us? So often it is with us, we find disappointing children, unkind relatives, ungrateful friends, loneliness, cherished hopes and plans brought to naught. All our earthly props are swept aside and we are forced to seek God. 'I saw the Lord',

'The things of earth grow strangely dim in the light of His Glory and Grace.' The Lord Jesus Christ brings salvation, hope, insight, courage and recovery. This is the eternal message for the weary and perplexed, a new vision centred in God, as we seek He comes to us in the shape that we need.

> The Lord is King! Lift up thy voice,
> O earth, and all ye heavens rejoice;
> From world to world the joy shall ring,
> 'The Lord omnipotent is King!'

Josiah Lander
1789

Day Thirteen

...who will go for us? Then said I, 'Here am I, send me.'

Isaiah 6:8

The New Testament has a story told by Jesus about two men who went into the Temple to pray. One said, 'I thank Thee that I am not as other men are', the second cried, 'God forgive me, a sinner'.

When we 'enter the Temple', we need to be spiritually hungry and sincere. There is a Church declaration: 'If we confess our sins, He is faithful and just to forgive, and to cleanse us from all unrighteousness.' Christ is our Saviour and is the sacrifice once offered for all. He bore our sin on Calvary's cross. His is our cornerstone, we build by faith on His finished work.

One line of a hymn is 'Fill Thou my life'; when this is claimed it can mean, 'take my life', my love life, my sex life, my Monday, Tuesday, Wednesday, Thursday... life. My work life, my office life, my school or kitchen life. My thoughts, desires, words and actions. This is taking a good look at ourselves and not at others in the light of the presence of God. When 'His train fills the Temple and He is on the Throne', the meaning is that He is in the whole world, East and West, First and Third World, rich and poor, haves and have nots, God for all to accept.

It is so easy, so very easy, to talk and speak glibly of these things, yet never to come face to face with reality and have no conception of what true faith implies. 'If any man be in Christ, he is a new creature and all things become new.'

Men and women in Christ will help to make a better world in their lives, enabling people to see what is wrong and endeavouring to put it right. 'What giving again,' I asked in dismay, 'and must I keep giving and giving away?' 'Oh no' said the Angel, whose eyes pierced me through, 'Just stop giving when God stops giving to you.'

Day Fourteen

Study to shew thyself approved unto God...

2 Timothy 2:15

We all have to learn. To eat, sleep, walk, play, dress, to handle money and people and so on, ad infinitum. Our characters good, bad, or indifferent affect other lives. When we apply for a job, a reference is usually required, not just a nice, *kind* generalisation in petty phrases, but the truth about us in action. What will our contribution be, are we trustworthy, honest, hard working, punctual, good mixers etc.?

This should be in strict confidence without placing the giver in a difficult position, with the disadvantage of knowing that we shall see it, either giving us an inflated impression of ourselves, or believing we have been unfairly treated and assessed!

Before a wise man marries a wife, he wants to know all about her, is she faithful, a good woman, and will she be a good mother? Wives, too, should be careful to make full enquiries into the characters of intended husbands.

A certain sailor took some seeds to Australia and sold them pretending they were a valuable plant. From these seeds the rascal sold, grew thousands and thousands of ugly useless dock weeds – a scourge causing endless trouble and annoyance. Weeds as seeds is a smart-alec story suiting the selfish ends and gains of many people today, doing the same in various ways. Actions good and bad have greater results than ever imagined.

Nursery rhymes often display great truths. 'This is the house that Jack built.' He only built the house but numberless consequences followed. The food store of malt, brought a rat, a cat to kill the rat, a dog, a cow, and a maiden all forlorn, a man all tattered and torn, a priest all shaven and shorn, and on and on. Actions do count.

The seasoned Apostle, Paul, urges the young man Timothy to study whether he will be worthy of the approval of His Creator. How? Just by accepting His gift in Christ as Saviour, friend and master. Then, in the power of the Holy Spirit, being enabled to live an honest, pure, good Christian life, built on a character that is the best, fitting him for a life on earth, and an eternal life to come in Heaven.

Day Fifteen

> They hid from the Lord God among the trees of the garden. But the Lord God called to the man, 'Where are you?'
>
> Genesis 3:8–9

Separation from God is a most sad thing. The first man to find this out was Adam. He was disturbed, realising with Eve, that they were naked. Ever ingenious, man soon solved that – just put together a few leaves to cover yourself and there is no need to worry any more. Then came from God the first question to Adam and Eve, his wife, hiding from the presence of the Lord who was walking in the garden in the cool of the day. 'Where art thou?' This potent question is directed to all mankind. To you and to me. Is our heart right? What is our relationship to the Creator? The first question in the New Testament is asked by men, 'Where is He?' Where do we seek to find Him? What is the answer for which we look and long? The choice is ours. As we go around seeking, we see a world hungry for pardon, hungry for justice, hungry for home and peace. Searching for the answer to the needs of individual lives and national lives. An Arctic explorer was asked whether, during eight months of slow starvation which he and his comrades had endured, they suffered much from pangs of hunger. 'No', he replied, 'we lost them in the sense of abandonment, in the feeling our countrymen had forgotten us and were not coming to rescue us. It was not until we were found and looked into other human faces that we realised how hungry we were.'

Day Sixteen

...the darkness is past, and the true light now shineth.

1 John 2:8

Many a river has to begin way up in the mountains, fighting its way through rock and clay, down through dark glens and dismal gorges. Twisting, winding, bending and turning until, at last, out into the sunlight and the open plain it flows peacefully into the sea. The River Severn begins on Plynlimnon and flows into the Bristol Channel. Going through the Woodhead Tunnel from Manchester to Sheffield, years ago – two or three miles of tunnel – the train lights often failed. The carriage would be in darkness and fill with smoke, very unpleasant to the traveller. Then the gleam of light would appear, the tunnel is finally reached with its end and pure air and sunlight. There *is* an exit to the tunnels of life, a way out. How does this come about, spiritually speaking? Our Lord Jesus Christ banishes the darkness; first of all from the face of God. That is why 'He came'. 'The darkness is passing and the real light already shines' (NEB). So the mystery was cleared; then what was God like? What were His real intentions towards men and women? Were there to be puzzles and mysteries of life, were hearts to be filled with fear? Does God really care? Is God the enemy or friend? Has God truly ever become fully human? In those far-off days, behind all they knew that someone was there, if only they could get a glimpse of His face. Then came Jesus, the knots were unravelled and life became real and worthwhile. The view through the clouds is then changed to a full one, the tunnel is ended, the light shines, the darkness is past. 'In the fullness of time, God sent forth His Son' (Galatians 4:4). The uncertainty is over. The works and message, the human life, death and Resurrection of Jesus prove it. This is our Lord Himself and the Holy Spirit, bringing and breaking God's very glory into our darkened hearts. It lies with us whether or not we accept this fact.

No sunbeam can exist without the sun; shut out the sun and it vanishes. Separate a soul from God and it is dead and lost, but with Christ there is light and life eternal.

Day Seventeen

> And Manoah prayed to the Lord, 'O Lord, I beg you, let the man of God come again to teach us how to bring up the boy who is to be born to us.'
>
> Judges 13:8

Nothing excels actual knowledge. What is the moon really like? Now men have been to see it, they took pictures, they brought back specimens, they walked around. They put it into words, now we know.

A simple man in the Old Testament, Manoah by name, and his wife were visited by an angel of God, who promised them an answer to their prayers. However, they were always in fear of heavenly visitors and had strange superstitions in those days. Manoah broke out in dismay saying, that because God had visited them, they would surely die. His wife was much wiser, she said in effect, 'If the Lord had meant to kill us, he would not have made us this kind promise.' In due time, a son, Samson, was born to them.

Christian people desire to thank God for the gift of His Son and for the deliverance from the hands of the great enemy, Satan. For the devotion of those who, down the ages, have stood between us and darkness, for the hope of a new and better world for all people, for the glorious hope of the Lord Jesus Christ's return. We must thank someone, and that is the person of God. Not merely an idea to be grasped but one whom we have to know as Saviour, Redeemer and friend.

Any thinking person will acknowledge that there still remains things in this world that are foul, ugly, sordid and base. What Jesus has done has enabled us to see these things as they are, we don't overlook them, they are real. Christ comes and opens our eyes.

A young man once found a paper money note in the street, and he never lifted his eyes from then onwards. Over the years, he collected buttons, coins, pins, a bent back and a poor disposition. He also lost the glory of sunlight, the night sky, the smiles of friends and the beauty of nature, and all the good things that life unfolds to us.

The message is; 'Look up, the darkness is passing and the true light is shining.'

Day Eighteen

...I will take heed to my ways...

Psalm 39:1

Surely God is in this place and I knew it not.

Genesis 28:16

Christian witness must reject the terribly low standards of today's society. Indeed, it must stand out in strong contrast. There needs to be integrity in marriage, which should be a sacred union before God and not a mere gratification of self and sex. In family relationships and responsibilities, there should be care for the old and infirm, the sick and weak minded; in work and business, club and church membership should be the best for all. Irresponsibility, desire for excitement and lack of consistent good living mar and spoil life. Deuteronomy 26:1–11 tells of what a man had to do in those far-off days. He watched for the first corn, vegetable or fruit, chose the finest and best, tended it carefully as it grew, and when it was ripe, he cut it, packed it with great care into a basket and carried it to the priest at the Temple Church. Here was a man who knew what he was doing: thanking the Creator and providing for the needs of others.

These observations can be illustrated by the story of a child. Little Sue stopped one night to stroke a kitten playing in the gutter. A man came up to her and spoke. What he said frightened her and she ran away. He followed her and she turned down an alley and hid in a dark corner. She listened to him searching for her and then going away. She ran home. Both parents were out, it was lonely and dark. She put herself to bed, covered by just a single blanket, and said her prayers. 'I was very frightened thinking of what had happened, I could not sleep,' she said. What was missing was a real home life, there were no mother's arms and loving words of comfort for her after such an experience. Despite a hard life, God was watching over Sue. His promise is; 'I am with you, I will keep you.'

Very often we miss and forget the blessings and presence of our Lord Jesus Christ. Many never acknowledge Him at all and, sadly, perhaps never will.

Day Nineteen

And they of Bethshemesh were reaping their wheat harvest in the valley: and they lifted up their eyes, and saw the ark and rejoiced to see it... and they sent messengers... saying, 'The Philistines have brought again the ark of the Lord; come ye down, and fetch it up to you.'

1 Samuel 6:13–21

Quite often when a crisis arrives in a person's life, they suddenly mention God and quote in vivid terms how events took a more happy way than their wildest thoughts. So be it. There are warnings, that the things and ways of God are never to be treated lightly, they have a rightful and proper place and are not for casual introduction.

The Philistines captured the ark of the Covenant from Israel but it brought endless trouble so they returned it to the Israelites.

On its return, the men of Bethshemesh lifted the lid and looked inside to see the gold idols sent with it. They were presumptuous and profane in their matter-of-fact ways and they perished. Later a new cart was sent for the ark to bring it to Jerusalem. At Nachan's threshing floors, the ark toppled as the cart moved over the rough floor, and the oxen stumbled. Uzzah put out his hand to steady the ark. He suddenly dropped dead; 'God smote him for his errors' (1 Chronicles 13:9–10). They were doing right things in the wrong way. The ark was designed with staves to be carried on the shoulders of men, not on a new cart.

Today, men and women strive to uphold a so-called toppling Christianity and make mistakes. Christ's religion does not require the self-efforts of folk to support it, especially in our individual lives. Jesus will never fail or falter, we need to shoulder our faith and march boldly onwards and forwards with peace and joy and with our Lord Jesus Christ always the very centre of our life and being.

Day Twenty

Acquaint now thyself with Him, and be at peace...

Job 22:21

A story is told of a castle in which lived an old man and his son. the castle was theirs, but they were penniless, and practically starving. Unknown to them, however, there was hidden in the castle some very valuable jewels, placed there by some ancestor to be used by any of his descendants in their time of need. For a long time, the old father and son went through great distress until, in some wonderful way, they learnt of the hidden treasure and their poverty was ended.

Spiritually speaking, many are living in places with hidden treasure close by, yet they continue to live in misery and distress. There is no reason why any child of God should not partake of the riches in the Glory of Christ; Jesus and the peace and joy of God which passes all understanding.

Not many people today stop to consider that in every one of us there are two parts. There is the obvious seen outer life. There is also the unseen inner life. The first may be defined in any age group, as may the second.

We tie ourselves to the externals of life and cling fondly to our outward possession. Our job, our home, family, relatives and friends. Today we may be surrounded by every material comfort, pleasure and security. Men and women greatly desire to ease and cure the stress and strain of life. We are constantly the targets of subtle suggestions and advertisements stating that we cannot be completely happy without this addition and that, so the desires for money and material benefits become now uppermost in mind. Those who claim only outward fleeting joys of the world are always restless, without true peace and find only disappointment in the end. Familiarity breeds contempt and possession brings indifference. The text says 'Acquaint now thyself with Him and be at peace.' Fix and fasten all your affections and desires on God. Make Him the end of all your longings. See Philippians 4:11–12.

Day Twenty-One

> ...Noah removed the covering of the ark, and looked, and, behold, the face of the ground was dry... and Noah went forth, and his sons, and his wife, and his sons' wives with him...
>
> Genesis 8:13–18

Every few years one reads of an expedition to the high mountains of Turkey to find evidence of Noah's ark. There is undoubted proof of a primeval flood thousands of years ago and this encourages belief in the Bible narrative of the ark. Three types of ark are referred to in the scriptures, the ark or floating cradle used to hide the baby Moses in the Nile bulrushes, and the ark or gilded chest of the Covenant. Dictionaries define 'ark' as a safe hiding or secreting place or a chest or ship. it is also symbolical of safety through God. The people of Noah's day forgot God, their ways were evil in His sight. The solitary exception was Noah *in* that world, but not *of* it, standing aloof when all around was sin and shame. He was 'at one' and walked with God, a singular example for Christian believers when trials, difficulties and temptations abound in the going-on all around. Suddenly the judgement of the Creator came to overtake men and women in their unpreparedness and folly. Noah built under God his ship, the ark. The Epistle of St Peter states, 'God waited for him.' (3:20). He and his family and animals went into the ark. 'God shut him in', the Bible states. The waters of judgement came in the universal flood, a world disaster. 'Then God remembered Noah', the floods subsided and the ark was grounded and a dove bore an olive branch. God said 'Go forth.' He was to begin a brave new world, to build the first altar in Scripture in praise and thanksgiving, to see the rainbow, a wonder and promise joining earth to Heaven. There was hope for the future, new life, new vision, new fellowship and faith with God. Noah's ark saved him from the judgement of God and is symbolical of the Saviour, the Lord Jesus Christ who, if we will, can be the ship of safety to sinners in need. A remarkable narrative indeed!

Day Twenty-Two

To Samuel a boy wearing a linen ephod.
Each year his mother made him a little robe and took it to him when she went up with her husband to offer the annual sacrifice...

1 Samuel 2:18–19

Let us love one another for love comes from God.

1 John 4:7

The Bible story of man begins with a father and mother; Adam and Eve. The Scriptures tell of several couples, good and bad; Abraham and Sarah. Ruth and Boaz. Ahab and Jezebel. Zacharias and Elizabeth, Joseph and Mary. Ananias and Sapphira.

In a world of power, one of the greatest powers is sex. Misuse of sex and power could be said to have brought about the downfall of the Greek and Roman Empires. A happy marriage does not require education on sexual techniques the marriage bed should be honourable. There should be physical, mental and spiritual union. It is not a matter of one forceful partner dominating life's scenes and keeping the other in some sort of unholy subjection. No, it is intended to be an ennobling influence, strengthening, maturing, encouraging and leading to lives and homes dedicated to the glory of the Creator. In such homes, parents can influence children to conduct lives of the very best. Love makes life happy, real and worthwhile. Christian love makes all the difference.

In the First World War, a padre knelt by a young, badly wounded soldier. 'I am thirsty,' said the soldier. The Minister gave him a drink. 'I am cold,' said the man; he gave him his coat. 'I am tired,' said the soldier; and he made him a pillow. 'Read to me now from the Book that causes a man to behave like you have to me,' said the dying soldier.

Day Twenty-Three

Whatsoever He tells you to do, do it.

> St John 2:5

We are all familiar with the term 'unconditional surrender'. We know that our late enemies, to end the war, had to give in to their victors in an uncalculating, complete surrender. The finest message for ourselves, and service, is the call to surrender to God and not seek to impinge our will and ways on Him for His benevolent approval. So, in the very first miracle which Jesus effected, we find that a surrender, a submission to His will was called for. Once the servants did this, a miracle was wrought. The water became wine. When we do the commands of Jesus unreservedly, then a miracle will take place in our lives. We shall be transformed, changed and guided for the better. Blessing will follow. Mary told the servants not to look to her for instructions but to have an eye to the Lord Jesus Christ. They were to have an ear also, to listen to what the Saviour had to say. They were called to action, to do without disputing or questioning, precisely as required. It was not an easy thing to give the wedding guests water when they called for wine. Yet because of their obedience, Christ turned the water into wine. Water pots, filled to the brim, immediately became changed into wine of the richest and best kind. Sparkling, strong in body, sweet in flavour, better in taste. Jesus, honouring marriage by His presence turned disgrace, concern and upset into happiness and joy for those who put their trust in Him, through faith. Because His will is good and perfect, it becomes acceptable to us in a glad and contented spirit. The door is closed I do not complain. The door is open I do not shrink to go through to new ways and opportunities.

> When morning fills the skies,
> My heart awaking cries,
> May Jesus Christ be praised!
> Alike at work and prayer,
> To Jesus I repair;
> May Jesus Christ be praised!

E. Caswall
1854

Day Twenty-Four

> I commend unto you Phoebe our sister... assist her in whatsoever business she hath need of you: for she hath been a succourer of many, and of myself also.
>
> Romans 16:1–2

This dear lady never dreamt that her name and way of life would be commended throughout the world for generations to come, in Holy Scripture. It tells of a life of selfless devotion not for herself but for others, a heart of love and kindness to those in need. Cenchrea was a small seaport adjoining the city of Corinth which was ill famed for its pagan, immoral ways of life. Men and women of doubtful origin and disrepute, the dregs of all nations passing through the city, where to be a Christian was no light task.

Phoebe's task was to take Paul's letter to the believers in Rome. This was the Apostle's most comprehensive declaration of the Gospel explaining the basic principles of Christianity and salvation by trusting in our Lord Jesus Christ, a message to go from the capital of the Roman Empire throughout the world. Paul, the Jew, Phoebe the Greek and the Roman friends were all to be fused together by the power of the Divine Love that melts the hearts of humanity. 'All one in Christ Jesus', brothers and sister in the Lord. It is this that matters most in the hearts, thoughts and lives of men and women.

Paul had been in Corinth a year or two, Phoebe had helped and succoured him, and now she was being asked, perhaps as a young woman, to undertake the arduous and dangerous journey to Rome. A journey of hundreds of miles by sea and road with great travelling dangers, usually undertaken by men only, a difficult, hair-raising experience The Lord Jesus Christ can fill our innermost being, cleanse us from all sin and shame of a self-centred life and give us, through the Holy Spirit, a life commendable to others as we help them. He alone can bind up the broken-hearted, make the unlovely, lovely, and the weakest strong.

'In as much as you have done it to others, you have done it unto me,' says our Lord.

> I've found a friend; O such a friend!
> He loved me ere I knew Him;
> He drew me with the cross of love,
> And He thus bound me to Him.

J.G. Small
1863

Day Twenty-Five

> Now Joshua was clothed with filthy garments, and stood before the angel.
>
> Zechariah 3:3

There was the High Priest in filthy clothes, standing before a spotless holy angel, with Satan at the side ready to accuse him, to read out his previous convictions. He has nothing to say – no answer. He carries his own sins and those of the people he represents, disquieting vision showing the great need of moral and spiritual reformation. God Himself comes to his aid, he is as a brand picked from the burning fire. There is to be a cleansing and robing of the glorious garments of the High Priest and a new mitre to set upon his head, he is to be cleansed, clothed and crowned. God's grace is spontaneous, free, no strings attached; generous, neither mean nor stinting. Grace is a prominent feature of the Christian faith. There is no grace in heathen religions. It means mercy for the undeserving, help for the helpless and hopeless, the unkind and the unthankful. Peace, joy and long-suffering, all met together in our Lord Jesus Christ (Ephesians 2:19).

How do I look now? We all love the thrill of a complete new rig-out. When others see the love of God in us, our lives will be the means of grace to them. We will be gracious in our dealings, anxious to avoid the spirit of hardness, hatred, severity. Anxious to show the spirit of love, patience, mildness, forgiveness and tenderness.

There is a true story of a West African man working as a conductor on a London bus. Collecting fares on the top deck, a gang of youths told him that the youths at the front deck would pay for all. Those there denied it and told him the youths at the rear would pay. Much verbal abuse followed about his colour. He was punched and pushed to the top of the stairs, then knocked down the stairs and kicked in the face causing him to lose an eye. His wife and family were told he was in hospital. His wife took the news calmly, she said she trusted in the Lord and their faith and testimony after ten years enabled them to forgive.

She said, 'If life was a bed of roses, there would be no need for God.' Happily, the case was taken up by a member of the House of Lords, who read the story in a national newspaper, pleading the cause of the coloured bus conductor. All were amazed that five thousand pounds came in small gifts, the greatest being thirty pounds. Strikingly sympathetic letters came from rich and poor, teenagers and pensioners. The Law dealt with the wrongdoers. God took care of the conductor and his family.

> Through the night of doubt and sorrow
> Onward goes the pilgrim band.

B.S. Ingemann
1825

Day Twenty-Six

Be self-controlled and alert. Your enemy the Devil prowls around like a roaring lion looking for someone to devour. Resist him standing firm in the faith.

1 Peter 5:8–9

If we endure, we will also reign with him.

2 Timothy 2:12

There is a story told of a London theatre with the stage, all set in brilliant footlights and a darkened audience; a bold man alone on the stage, and soft eastern music and charm. Slowly over the stage comes a mighty python moving to and fro, to and fro, entirely in the control of the snake charmer. The climax comes as the snake gently coils itself around the man's body and uncoils, as the audience applauds. Once more the reptile glides sinuously around the charmer's body and once more unwinds its powerful length. Louder and louder the people clap and cheer. Finally the python moves a third time round and round the man. Then, above the applause is heard a terrifying piercing death shriek, the crunching and cracking of flesh and bones. A tragedy has happened, the very beast that was to be charmed and played with so long and so easily, has become the master.

This could be a graphic illustration of the ways and power of Satan when a man or woman play with temptation and sin and are in bondage to them. It is so vivid and true, as we all know.

Selfishness, envy, greed, temper, passion, lust and so on, can take over, so that they cannot be thrown off and they dominate life itself.

The Scriptures are full of warnings such as these and tell us that the Lord Jesus Christ has promised to break the powers and chains of sin. When events bring trouble, depression, loneliness, fear and ill treatment by others, Christ alone can bring to us assurances peace, joys and true lifelong blessings as we have faith in Him.

Day Twenty-Seven

> [Jesus said,] 'And when these things begin to come to pass, then look up and lift your heads; for your redemption draweth nigh.'
>
> St Luke 21:28

Sometimes, we hear the cry, 'Britain has lost its Great.' With this goes a sad and sombre mood. Insecurity, fear, anxiety, disillusionment, a kind of hopelessness, helplessness and sense of powerlessness. Not merely social and political problems in a narrow sense but the broad and penetrating sense of the fellow human condition and the corresponding crisis. Morale and morals are so low as to touch the bottom. Beliefs and faith are so weak as to snap. 'They', whoever 'They' are, have taken over control. Big business, unions, local and central Government, bureaucracy, the media, TV, radio and press are all conspiring against us.

Family ways of life are now rapidly eroding, with the corresponding fall in educational standards and rise in delinquency. History sets before us the collapse of great empires and civilisations by similar tragic patterns – destruction from the very heart gone rotten inside. Today we have loss of national pride, greed, drunkenness, violent and heartless crimes; all set against days of luxury holidays and travel, costly foods, furniture, shoes, clothing, trivialised music and entertainment and so on.

You say to me, 'What can we do? Where do we begin?' The starting point lies with Christian people. Are we prepared to stand up and be counted? – it will cost – it won't be easy! The call is to exercise all the influence we can in every possible way to bring in the Kingdom of God and create better lives for men and women.

Our Lord Jesus Christ said 'Ye are the salt of the earth – Ye are the light of the world.' He also says 'Come unto me, all ye that are weary and heavy laden, and I will give you rest.' Then He adds further, 'Go ye into all the world and make disciples in the name of the Father, Son, and the Holy Spirit.'

Two men were walking past a church with a weather vane on the steeple, inscribed with the words, 'God is Love'. 'How strange,' said the first, 'does it mean that God's love can vary with the wind?'

'Oh no,' said the second, 'It means that God is Love, whichever way the wind is blowing – even when the storm blows strong.'

> Who is He in yonder stall,
> At whose feet the shepherds fall?
> 'Tis the Lord! O wondrous story!
> ...Crown Him, Lord of all.

> B.R. Hanby
> 1866

Day Twenty-Eight

The hour has come for you to wake up from your slumber... The night is nearly over – the day is almost here.

Romans 13:11–12

It is not always easy to wake up, some need a terrific lot of waking in the morning. So with spiritual lethargy – soul slumber. We are told Satan lulls men and women to sleep, doing his best to make us and keep us apathetic and indifferent to the things of God. 'Knowing the season – that now it is high time to awake.'

What season? the era – the end of the age when, as in the words of Jesus, 'You will hear of wars, rumours of wars, tribulations, famines, distress of nations, men's hearts failing them for fear.' Yes, in our own age and day. the night is the whole period of alienation from the Creator, we need to 'cast off the works of darkness', the deeds of the old man in us, self-centredness, moral evils, lying, deceit, encumbrances and besetting sins, all those things that mar and spoil life. Cast them off: cast – a violent word, tear off – demanding immediate decision, complete resolution, getting rid of them.

There is the sad expression 'Dead as a dodo'. this was an enormous turkey-like bird with absurdly small legs and wings. The last died about two hundred years ago in Mauritius. Settlers noticed it had a lazy time, had no need to fly – so it didn't. No need to run – so it didn't. The legs grew shorter, the wings weaker. The Portuguese called it 'Dodo' which can be interpreted 'idiot' and the bird soon became a lost species and a proverb.

When we wake up to our situation, what must we do? St Paul says, 'put on the armour of light.' This is the 'Helmet of Salvation, the breastplate of righteousness, the shield of faith, the sword of the spirit, the sandals of the Gospel of peace.' So may we wake and not sleep. In our Lord Jesus Christ, live and not die.

> Brightly gleams our banner,
> Pointing to the sky,
> Waving on Christ's soldiers
> To their home on high.

T.J. Potter
1860

Day Twenty-Nine

> For the creation was subjected to frustration, not by its own choice, but by the will of one who subjected it, in hope that the creation itself will be liberated from its bondage to decry and brought into the glorious freedom of the children of God.
>
> Romans 8:20–21

Over recent years the age of compulsory school leaving has been gradually raised because the conditions of life in our modern industrial society present many problems. It is indeed difficult to know how best to assist young people. There are times when employers are competing fiercely for juveniles and there are times when school leavers cannot find a job. The trend is to command high wages and dismiss thoughts of unemployment. Some are unsatisfactory or indolent and experience five or six jobs in two or three years after leaving school. Every time real hard duties or disciplines assert themselves, they leave to find another job. On the other hand, the population is getting older and older people are sticking and hanging on to responsible places making promotion for others difficult. A sense of frustrated employment leads to most unfortunate mental attitudes, as does unemployment.

There is something of this, too, in the ways of nations setting the poorest peoples against the richest in the world. Only when God is brought into the lives of people and nations, can much of the theories and practices reshape our country in terms of worthwhile living and learning. Christianity is social because it compels us to be concerned about the world in which we live.

The message is: share your joys, hopes and beliefs and seek to better the lot of those around and those in far-off places. Open to them the treasures of God, to free them from the bondage of decay and bring them into the glorious freedom of the people of God.

Day Thirty

> From that time on, this disciple took her to his own home.
>
> St John 19:27

An important influence in the life of Christ was his work and workshop. He was a carpenter in Nazareth. He found time for honest labour. Workshops are for producing, and above all, for making men and women. The joiner's shop helped to make the Saviour. He worked as unto his Father. All work, no matter what it is, is sacred. Housework, school work, shop work, office work, farm work, factory work. The yokes of Jesus would be well made, well fitting, light and easy for the cattle. So, said Jesus, are the yokes of His followers. Our daily round and common task, every endeavour, should not be a drudgery. If it is, Christ can change it.

The home of Jesus was also a tremendous influence upon Him. He was the eldest of a large family (Matthew 13:55). His father, Joseph, probably died fairly early. It was a good home and a poor home, typical of its day and age. The various sayings of Jesus reflect incidents of his home life. The search for a lost coin, the lighting of candles, the measuring of the flour and leaven, the feeding of the children and so on. Christ found time for his home, his mother and his friends, at the wedding of Cana, and at Calvary's Cross (St John 19:25–27).

What is home to you? Don't neglect your own hearth, parents and friends. There can be great temptations to engage oneself elsewhere but remember home should be the best and sweetest place of all. Do what you can to make it so.

> Cast care aside, lean on thy guide,
> His boundless mercy will provide.

J.S.B. Monsell
1863

Day Thirty-One

> He did not say anything to them without using a parable. But when he was alone with his own disciples, He explained everything.
>
> St Mark 4:34

There is an obvious influence of the love of nature in the life of our Lord Jesus Christ. The birds nesting, the shepherding of the sheep, the vine and the fig tree. He spoke of the lilies in their glory and the golden miracle of the harvest, the mystery of the unfolding buds; the lakeside and the fishing scenes. Jesus found time for the things of nature around Him. Do we? What do we know of the beauty and revelation of God in the things of life before our eyes?

More than this, Jesus found time for human nature. He speaks of children growing sulky at play, of women pestering the magistrates, the prodigal son and his wayward ways, the religionists of His day on parade, the jealous disciple and the thief among them. Widows, the rich, the poor, the sick, the lepers, blind, deaf, dumb, lame and dying – all are mentioned. Through the tragedy, sin, comedy and foibles of life and its shameful consequences, Jesus loved men and women as God alone could. He found time for them. Do we? Or do we just live our own selfish lives? Perhaps we might here also remind ourselves that we should find time for ourselves. Our bodies need care, our clothes, appearance and health. We need seasons of leisure and recreation. We need to be at ease, to stop posing and posturing, being irritable and restless. Find time for yourself, you are the only one of your kind.

God created everyone absolutely unique, each of us with a precious sacred personality. Be yourself, be true, realise the responsibility of life. Young people especially, cultivate, improve and develop yourself.

It is vital what we say, it is more vital what we do. It is most vital what we are. Ask the Holy Spirit of life to fill you with the Grace of God.

> Breathe on me, Breath of God,
> Fill me with life anew.

E. Hatch
1898

'Find time for God,' said the Abbot to Brother Jerome as he hurried around. 'Vigils and fastings are not God, Matins and Vespers are not God, Service in the Choir or School, Library or Church, are not God.'

These things may lead to Him or may stem away from Him. But it is only in Him, that thou canst live the life that is life indeed! Make it your chief duty to walk with Him. Let everything lead to Him. Let nothing come between your soul and His very Self. 'Find time for God.' Later the same young man himself became the Abbot, revered and beloved by all, and often repeating with gratitude the precious charge he himself had once received – 'Find time for God'.

Day Thirty-Two

> Love not the world, neither the things that are in the world.
>
> 1 John 2:15

What is it that spoils our lives today? What is the most grievous problem facing the people and nation? Surely the undoubted answer in almost every case is 'the world'. By this term 'world', we mean that part of society organising itself without God. God and Mammon cannot mix. All around us are evidences of the devastating onslaught of the horror called Mammon; there is constant clamour to take the brake off, but once the moral restraints are relaxed, the dangers are very great. Today, materialism is a gripping thing.

The lust of the flesh gives a desire to indulge. The lust of the eyes gives a desire to covet and possess. The pride of life gives a desire to attract. This swagger of life covers an immense field. Our homes, our car, our dress, our pose, our words, our make-up, our table and so on. John Bunyan tells of a man 'who could look no way but downwards, with a muck-rake in his hand. There stood also one over his head with a celestial crown in his hand, and proffered him that crown, for his muck-rake, but the man did neither look up nor regard, but raked to himself the straws, the small sticks and the dust of the floor.'

Is this a picture known to us? Please do not think we are getting at you, we know nothing of your personal life, it is yours, your very own. God alone knows each of us. The touchstone is simply this: our passion and personal love for Him. Whether things are wrong or even appear on the surface to be right, we can be very, very clear, if they take the fine edge off our devotion: if they cause the flame in our heart to flicker out or lessen our vision of the Saviour, our Lord Jesus Christ, then they need to be kept out of our life. 'The world passeth away, and the lusts thereof, but he that doeth the will of God abideth for ever.'

Day Thirty-Three

> Seek first His Kingdom and His righteousness and all things will be given unto you as well. Therefore, do not worry about tomorrow for tomorrow will worry about itself.
>
> St Matthew 6:33–34

What a strange world it would be if others before us had not done something to prepare for those coming later. Imagine life with no roads paved, no drains, just stench, floods and deep mud. No lights, just darkness at night. Nowhere to learn; no schools; no library, no books, no post. Others have worked and we have enjoyed the fruits of their labours.

Many years ago, a king of Judah called Jehoiachin was defeated in battle and taken captive to Babylon. He remained captive for thirty-seven years. In time a new king reigned over Babylon and he had mercy on Jehoiachin. He brought him out of captivity and he spoke kindly to him. He made him pre-eminent over other captive kings. His clothes were changed, he put on royal robes once more. He became the friend and companion of the king who set him free. He lived in the palace and received a daily allowance which was to extend to the rest of his life. What lesson has this Bible truth for us? Are we bound by the chains and fetters of our sins? Maybe we have been held prisoner a long, long time, perhaps in the grip of some bad habit or foul way. Today here and now, our benefactor – the King, the Lord Jesus Christ – comes Himself to us, if we are willing, to set us free, cleanse our sins, put off the chains of Satan, our selfishness, our lies, our deceit and all the ugly things that blight and spoil our living. Jesus Christ, the Son of God, left Heaven and came to this earth to live and die for you and me. He was perfect and came to show us God's love and to take our burdens. He speaks by His Spirit. He begins to bless us and use our lives so that others will know we are changed, not our wearing apparel but the things which make up our character, our thoughts, our words, our deeds, our very selves. Jesus will honour us, He will be with us each day. He will make us a 'daily allowance' for the rest of our lives here on earth and then we shall be with Him in Heaven. Although our trials and difficulties are sometimes very great and tiresome yet because Jesus is our Saviour, friend and master, He can give us power and strength to conquer, and our text thus becomes very real.

Day Thirty-Four

...it is not in man that walketh to direct his steps.

Jeremiah 10:23

It has been said that after the blitz of Coventry, in the cathedral lay a burnt cross showing two words, 'Father forgive'. With the rebuilding, the architects' vision can be summed up in these words: relevance (does it meet the need?); reconciliation (does it bring together?); resurrection (does it bring new life?). The same can be said of the rebuilding of the German city of Dresden, blitzed by the Allies. The Apostles and the early church had the same aim. The Holy Spirit enabled them to go forward through persecution, privation and death, with genuine joy and peace. This gave them boldness and fearlessness, unafraid of what might come tomorrow. the fruits of the Spirit were seen in their lives – which were rich and full. Showing love, peace, long-suffering, kindness, goodness, faithfulness, meekness and self-control. These were the qualities which made the men and women down the ages noted for the best and finest lives.

We cannot do these things in our own strength alone. We need to be restored like the lame beggar in Acts 3 to give the glory to God, truly worshipping Him in our hearts and living, witnessing to the world at large, being filled with spiritual power and joy from above. We must be ready to enrich the lives of others. Remember we are not at our own disposal, but under a divine direction. A day's happenings are often overruled so as to be quite contrary to our expectations.

Day Thirty-Five

> I tell you the truth, anyone who gives you a cup of water in my name because you belong to Christ will certainly not lose his reward.
>
> St Mark 9:41

Every now and then, disaster shakes the world. Epic illustrations include the unexpected sinking of the liner *Titanic* on her maiden voyage, the earthquake in Kobe, Japan, the plane returning USAF soldiers and families to Vietnam which crashes in Alaska, a tidal wave in Pakistan and a bridge in Canada which collapses sweeping commuters, holidaymakers and passers-by to sudden death. Our lives are lived out in the tension between what has happened and what will happen, between the present tangible world and the unknown future of the world to come. The whole truth of history will be revealed as accomplishing the purpose of God. Is there any real hope beyond the grave?

Many people prefer to do the judging and to do it now. They remain unaccountable to anyone. They decide the rights and wrongs, the truths and falsehoods of life: all very human with a place for unity, tolerance, charity and better world conditions.

God and eternity have no place in their assessments. The Christian Gospel is entirely different. Our lives are of paramount importance to our Creator, and He will require an account of them (Romans 14:12). Even the visiting of the sick and prisoners – the giving of a cup of water will not go unnoticed. What we do to one another, we do to Jesus Christ, our Lord, who cares for each one of us who trust in Him.

Day Thirty-Six

[Jesus said,] 'Have faith in God.'

St Mark 11:22

Before the last war, we often read of a newspaper mystery man at the seaside. Anyone challenging him and showing him a copy of the paper received a prize. He was everywhere, but people missed him. On the beach, on the promenade, at the bandstand, in the main street, at the station or car park. The Lord Jesus Christ is about too. He is not a mystery man, but He seeks to be recognised and sought out, especially by His followers. He has a rich prize – Eternal Life. We are often called upon to make our witness in the world as true believers. Our Christianity may be a seven-day week experience or simply a religion of convenience. It can be a full trust and faith in God or something falling far, far short of what He would have us to be. A porter had a little dog tied to a platform lamp-post. 'Why so?' asked a traveller. 'He's chewed his label,' came the reply. Is this our case too? Are we prepared to wear the label daily, or do we chew it up every Monday morning? Have faith in God.

All real believers in our Lord Jesus Christ know what they believe and the power of the Holy Spirit works in their lives. 'He that believeth on the Son of God has the witness in him.' (1 John 5:10).

The Churches may fail, the Cross of Christ cannot fail, neither in the West or the East. Christ is the hope of mankind and whether we are drawn to Him or not, He alone reveals the life for which men and women are longing. This is the Gospel which meets the needs of mankind, just as your front door key fits the lock! Jesus said, 'Have faith in God.'

Day Thirty-Seven

> ...I being in the way [i.e. the trodden path] the Lord led me...
>
> Genesis 24:27

Our decisions in life are often based on imperfect human knowledge and mixed with feelings. As the years go by we should become more understanding and patient. We see the mosaic jigsaw of life fitting into place to constitute the true picture and will of the Creator. It is not that to which we must be resigned, rather is it that to which we should be happily reconciled. St Paul declares that the will of God is always good, always perfect, always acceptable. Dante wrote, 'His will is our peace.' How then may we know God's will for us? By constant and careful study of the Holy Scripture. There we see in general terms those things which He is likely to approve. By examining our own circumstances, we seek in them indications of God's plans and purposes. Look for harmony and avoid discord.

The Holy Spirit will relate things to us and make plain to heart and mind those things we ought best to do, not a seeking of God's consent for our decisions but a true heart yielding to find His way for us, leaving it to Him to tighten or loosen the reins.

It is misguided to consult daily horoscopes, so-called messages from the stars! What do these mean? 'Take mental inventory; vitamins and body care should result in glowing appearance. Outward facades count now'; or 'Limelight beckons (but can also scorch). Be cautious about speech and actions. Background manoeuvres are wiser.' So says the horoscope!

Far better to read and pray. 'Keep me from being false to Thee and graciously direct me. I will obey Thee eagerly as Thou dost open up my life... lead me in Thine obedience for it is my joy' (Psalm 119:29–35, Moffatt's translation).

Day Thirty-Eight

The Lord is my Shepherd... He leadeth me...

Psalm 23:1–2

So too, by no mechanical process but by some great mysterious privileges, we, if we are honestly seeking God's way, will find ourselves automatically on the right path led by God. You might ask 'How am I to know when this is so?... I am ready to obey if I could only be sure that it is His voice and command I hear.' Reading the Scriptures and quiet prayer will tune us in to His wavelength. Reason and listen to your own conscience, thinking of the circumstances of your life. Have I been willing to let go every known sin or inconsistency? Am I maintaining right relationships with my family, friends and fellow creatures? Am I willing to make restitution for wrongs committed? Am I absolutely honest, true and unselfish? Have I the love of God in my heart? Does my way go counter to the highest standard of belief I already possess, does it contradict the revelations which our Lord Jesus Christ gives to us?

There is a story of an English merchant who, passing through an eastern slave market, was much moved at heart by the scenes. At great cost to himself he bought a slave in order to set him free. During the transaction, the slave misunderstood the man's intention and indignantly denounced him, amazed that he, a Briton should purchase a slave.

'I have bought you,' said the merchant, 'To set you free.'

Then falling at his feet in sobs and tears, the poor slave cried out, 'You have taken my heart captive – I am your willing slave for ever.' We, too, are bought with a price, the precious blood of our Lord Jesus Christ. Are we then willing to be His 'slave for ever?'

Day Thirty-Nine

> ...the soul of the people was much discouraged because of the way.
>
> Numbers 21:4

This was said of the people of Israel freed from slavery in Egypt but wandering in the wilderness, before finding the Promised Land. The same is often true in life especially today. Joshua said to the Israelites, 'Let there be a good space of vacant ground between you and the guiding ark, that you may know by which way you ought to go.' Joshua 3:4.

Don't press precipitately on the heels of half-disclosed providences, or you will be uncommonly apt to mistake the road. To secure the guidance real from God; ask for it, work for it, follow it. Many Christians are like Nelson. They put the telescope to the blind eye, when the flag is flying at the Admiral's peak signalling, 'Come out of action'. They are then determined to do their own thing and stay where they are. There are far too many blind, deaf and dumb Christians about today, naturally, 'much discouraged because of the journey'. Pray for the evidence of God, the revealing of God, and the showing forth of God in your ways.

Day Forty

> Because of his great love for us, God, rich in mercy, made us alive with Christ even when we were dead in transgressions – it is by grace you have been saved.
>
> Ephesians 2:4–5

There has recently been an attempt to put the Gospel message into every home by the distribution of a booklet. Sad to say, failure came partly because the cost was too great and also because people regarded it as part of the junk mail in their daily letter box. Something totally irrelevant to today and only fit for the litter bin!

This contributes to the notion that in our land today and in the future, the Christian faith and Church is fading faster and faster, heading towards an eventual demise similar to that of the ill-fated tiger.

This, one of the most beautiful of the great mammals, we are told, is also now approaching extinction. Named for its fast pace, the Medes, Greeks and Persians called an arrow 'tigris' for its speed. Furthermore, the River Tigris is so named because it is one of the most rapid flowing. Hence the name tiger for its animal speed, strength and cunning. Eastern cultures have attached to the animal some kind of veiled magic. Their traditional medicines seek the skins, bones, claws and so on of the beast for a now thriving industry, so that the days of the tiger are being depleted to a point of no return.

As far as the Christian faith and Church is concerned, it can never fail especially so in the life of a believer true to Christ. Pray for a lively, active, obedient faith, counted for righteousness, then despair will be swept away. The mercy and grace of God will take over.

> What a friend we have in Jesus
> All our sins and griefs to bear;
> What a privilege to carry
> Everything to God in prayer

J.M. Scriven
1855

Day Forty-One

The disciples said 'Lord, teach us to pray.'

St Luke 11:1

Being a Mancunian, I visited Manchester Cathedral on a blazing hot summer's day. It was dusty out of doors, the windows were dirty and drab. However, inside the windows there shone a riot of sunlit colour, beauty of design and a majesty of pictorial suggestion. We never can tell, until we enter into a personal inside experience. So it is with prayer. An atheist Russian lady boasted with a touch of hauteur, 'We never pray'. A negative experience, complete and final indeed.

On the other hand, a humble Christian soul experiences God in prayer and grows expert by experiment. The more she prays, the more she wants to pray. Prayer belongs to the supernatural, it cannot be explained. Arguments and discussions confuse, experiment persuades: 'Lord, teach us to pray'. It has been said, a Christian on his knees sees further than a philosopher on his toes.'

The disciples had prayed before imperfectly, then they saw and heard Jesus, and it made all the difference. Jesus never disputed the value of prayer; He prayed, just as He never argued for the existence of God. Prayer is the life blood in the veins, it is the very breath of the soul. It is an experience, something above and beyond doubt.

The praying Christ is the supreme testimonial for prayer. He taught prayer, He had a prayer habit – daily, varied, in all the great crisis times. There was fellowship with the Father, thanksgiving, petition for his own needs, intercession for the needs of others. Tired? Yes, often. Praying 'all through the night' (St Mark 6:46); 'a great while before day' (St Mark 1:35); 'amid the crowds during the day' (St Mark 7:34). There were also many times of private prayer unknown and unrecorded. 'Lord, teach us to pray.'

> Lord, teach us how to pray aright,
> With reverence and with fear;
> Though dust and ashes in Thy sight,
> We may, we must, draw near.

J. Montgomery
1818

Day Forty-Two

Pray without ceasing.

1 Thessalonians 5:17

Life is full of moods, and these affect our prayers; joy, sorrow, smiles, tears, unbelief, doubt, fear, weariness, forgetfulness. Sometimes we are too preoccupied, sometimes too tired. When such moods come in, our love for God and to God is weakened. These late twentieth century days are full of life's stresses and bustles, but read of the days of the Lord Jesus Christ; if any days were full, surely it was those of the Master.

There is no substitute for prayer, it is a serious business. Jesus prayed 'with strong crying and tears.' Energy of mind, heart, body and soul is required. There must be absolute honesty with ourselves and others. Sin must be dealt with: 'only the pure in heart see God'. There must be no insulators breaking contact. The psalmist said, 'If I regard iniquity in my heart, the Lord will not hear me,' (66:18).

A certain minister was disturbed by a shabby old man going each day, at noon, into his church and coming out again after a few minutes. The clergyman asked the caretaker to question the old man. He said, 'I go in to pray – can't say a long prayer, so I just comes in and says 'Jesus, it's Jim, I wait a minute then I leave.' Soon after, news came that Jim had been injured and was in hospital, and people said he had a wonderful influence in the ward. Grumbling patients forgot to grouse about the ward and the food, the nurses and one another, and so on. It became a merry, cheerful place, ringing with laughter. 'Well Jim,' said the Sister to him one day, 'The men say you are responsible for the change in the ward – they say you are always happy.'

'Yes, Sister, I am,' said Jim. 'You see, it's my visitor. Every day He makes me happy.' 'Your visitor?' The Sister had never seen a visitor come to see the lonely old man. 'When does he come?' 'Every day,' said Jim. 'He comes at twelve and stands at the foot of the bed, and He smiles at me and says, "Jim – it's Jesus."'

> Prayer is the soul's sincere desire,
> Uttered or unexpressed;
> The motion of a hidden fire,
> That trembles in the breast.

J. Montgomery
1818

Day Forty-Three

[Jesus said,] 'All things, whatsoever ye shall ask in prayer, believing, ye shall receive.'

St Matthew 21:22

Continuing our thoughts on prayer, there is a little verse, 'I often say my prayers, but do I ever pray.' Doubt and unbelief cause us to ask serious questions. Is prayer just a self-satisfying sop? Surely events would turn out the same, whether we prayed or not. What proof is there that our prayers are answered, is it any use? Am I just groping after God? We expect immediate answers, we give up and turn away if they do not come.

Against all this, prayer is said to be the heart of true religion. After the vision of our Lord Jesus Christ in the Transfiguration, He descended the mountain to find His disciples being derided because they could not heal a dumb man. Beaten and baffled they asked Him, 'Why could we not cast the devil out?' Jesus replied, 'This kind can come forth by nothing but by prayer,' (St Mark 9:29). The Scriptures reveal many prayers for many occasions.

There is no alternative for it; finally on the Cross, Jesus said, 'Father, into Thy hands I commend my Spirit.' He died praying, 'Father, forgive them.'

At the time of the Crimean War, the wounded needed hospital care on the spot. It was soon discovered that forty per cent of the soldiers admitted, died of diseases acquired in the hospital. Florence Nightingale embraced the task of putting things right. Poor sanitation and hygiene, bad, inedible food, shortage of medicines and surgical supplies needed attention. She insisted on the proper laundering of the bedding, better food, unblocked sewers and confidence in doctors and staff. The source of water contamination was traced to a dead horse lying in the stream supplying the hospital. She had the carcass removed and sanitation vastly improved. Within six months the deaths had fallen dramatically.

The whole essence is that when things are wrong they must be put right. Prayer changes things. The shortest prayer in the Bible is that of an ethnic mother to Jesus for her daughter, 'Lord, help me'. This may be yours too.

> Fill thou my life, O Lord my God,
> In every part with praise,
> That my whole being may proclaim
> Thy being and Thy ways.

H. Bonar
1866

Day Forty-Four

> Lord to whom shall we go? Thou has the words of eternal life. And we believe and are sure that Thou art that Christ, the son of the Living God.
>
> St John 6:68–69

It could be said that there is far too much clutter and wrong ideas of trust and thought amongst people today. Let me put it to you, have you a true conviction of the real Christian faith in your life? Is your personal faith feeble and faint, giving those outside the impression that in the end nothing really matters very much anyway?

Is the question of facing up to whether one believes or not, an individual decision of small consequence How wrong. These are tremendous issues, on these choices hangs the background of an eternity – of an eternal life divinely prepared for each and everyone. Today the trumpet gives an uncertain sound, muffled and confused; Jesus Christ is played down and a materialistic world predominates. What about the superficial questioning of the Scriptures as the Word of God? The cynical and sceptical attitudes towards the Gospels? All the negative statements that mar and spoil faith? The world plans everything to be comfortable, cocooned in good pay, pensions and pleasant surroundings.

Some would say wrongly, the real world of hardship, suffering and evils, human situations and tragedies, deprivation and wretchedness must be swept under the carpet and kept away beyond reach. Government, science, humanism and politics may eventually be able to come up with the answer! Yes, there is a great need for true Christian conviction and commitment, with a willingness to stand up and be counted. How is it with each of us? The very important passage in our text shows us that in those far-off days, the disciples were concerned too, and the truth was dawning upon them.

> In full and glad surrender
> I give myself to Thee;
> Thine utterly and only,
> And evermore to be.

F.R. Havergal
1873

Day Forty-Five

Whom say ye that I am?

St Matthew 16:15

This is the turning point in the ministry of our Lord Jesus Christ. He is alone with His disciples and puts this question to them. Humanly, it is conceivable that by degrees a full understanding of His mission had dawned upon them. He was the son of God. he kept it close, the sick when healed, were asked not to publish it, the evil spirits who shouted it aloud were condemned to silence. he is Alpha and Omega, the first and the last – the light of the world. Today, people class together the great thinkers and leaders of the world, Buddha, Confucius, Mohammed, Socrates, Plato, Gandhi, Jesus Christ. Is that so? Is he merely one of many: St Francis, St Augustine, St Bernard, Jesus? No! Christianity is not just another 'also ran'. Educationalists and humanists may say so, we must not. All others fail to meet the human need, Jesus does not fail. This is a personal challenge. To the Samaritan woman at the well; to Thomas the doubter; to Peter the denier; to Pontius Pilate, the governor; to Mary Magdalene, possessed by seven devils; Saul of Tarsus, the persecutor; the question comes, 'What do you think?' To all of us, this question is confronting us in three ways. By history – who can He be? By the Bible – who can He be? By our very consciences, who can He be? There is no escape from this question. Simon Peter gave the answer and it was correct. His own personal, startling, tremendous answer, 'Thou are the Christ, the Son of the Living God.'

Peter saw, in Jesus, the longed-for Messiah, the Saviour of the world. Someone who would be the hope of the world. The answer to every prayer. The solid rock in a shifting world built on sand. Peter felt like that because he was living with Jesus, who had called him with a simple 'Follow Me'. Now he was following and realised it. God deals with problems and shattered futile lives. Peter saw lives being changed and remade. Only God could do this. he saw his own life changed, sins forgiven and power to conquer sin and be, 'born again'. Jesus does for me what only God can do: 'Thou are the Christ,' he said.

Day Forty-Six

He hath done all things well...

St Mark 7:37

Here is the Scriptures in the narrative of the healing of a deaf and dumb man. Born deaf, he also stammered with his tongue: he was one who could scarcely be understood, and who it was hard to make understand. A very sad case. So much so, that others had to speak up for him. 'They besought Jesus to put His hand upon him.' In other words, to give him the usual treatment, but Jesus did more – much more – He always does! he took the man aside from the crowd, to make him more receptive, to lessen the counter-attractions of people and the world around. It is good to be alone with Christ, in the quietness, maybe in the sickroom, in some sad bereavement, in sorrow, in loneliness, in the aftermath of sin, just yourself, your very own soul, taking quiet stock.

Next, Jesus gave the man of Himself. His own fingers, His own spittle, touching the ears, and tongue of the deaf and dumb. He always gives of Himself, as on the Cross of Calvary, to call who will gladly accept Him.

He looked to Heaven, His power was from above, the same power which we may have and share. He sighed. The very heart of Christ went out in pity. Here was a soul far removed from the glorious humanity first conceived in Adam.

A man, blighted and suffering, in separation from his Creator. he spoke, 'be opened' – all was well. The deaf heard, the dumb could now speak. If we desire and let Him, our Lord Jesus Christ can open – open our minds, open our eyes, open our hearts, and we are astonished beyond measure. 'He hath done all things well.' We cannot keep silent, there is unspeakable joy, hope and power in our hearts.

> The strife is o'er, the battle done;
> Now is the victor's triumph won;
> O let the song of praise be sung;
> Alleluia.

F. Pott
1859

Day Forty-Seven

> ...continue in the faith, grounded and settled, and be not moved away from the hope of the Gospel which ye have heard...
>
> Colossians 1:23

We are constantly told today of the widespread decline in moral standing and standards. This includes juvenile crime, together with a terrific increase in divorce, with fornication and adultery rampant. Sadly, family life and the welfare of young people, especially children, have become badly affected, with a decline of truthfulness and personal honesty.

Not the least in these matters are present-day atheism and agnosticism, coupled with multi-racialism. Many folk are only interested in 'What is in it for me?' so greed and selfishness becomes dominant.

When Gregory saw the fair-haired youthful British slaves in the Roman slave market many years ago, although they could not speak to him, their very bearing and faces cried out to him. 'These are angels not Angles,' he remarked and sent his aide, St Augustine, to England with the Gospel message. Today perhaps more than for many years, Britain's cry is going up, 'Lord, help us'. The answer rests with each individual; every believer can help in all places and at all times, ready to confess our Lord Jesus Christ, His Gospel and what He has done for us and can do in our lives and in our Land.

Day Forty-Eight

I have made and I will bear; even I will carry...

Isaiah 46:4

In some countries abroad, as we wend our way through the town, we may suddenly come upon a great procession. Obviously it is a religious procession and there go before us, idols, banners and texts in profusion. The whole street is filled with a tawdry, tottering mass. You ask what is the meaning of this? 'Oh,' comes the reply, 'they do this here, they are carrying their religion.' You see not only the beautiful figures and idols but peeping below, underneath the placards, you see, to your amazement, that the whole scene is carried on the bent and jostling shoulders of men. Men, whose perspiring faces and sweating brows appear to be labouring with a great burden.

As we consider the country we expect that this religion is the secret of the land's greatness. Instead, we are told how poor and downtrodden the people are. Indeed, not many years past, the place was torn apart by a bloody and bitter civil war.

Natives of these places will tell us that they know of our land too, of its victory in world wars, the rich oil prize, the high Western standards of business and civil life together with its so-called 'Christian' ways. Now they tell you there are new gods called democracy, social security, freedom for all, easy optimism, and so on, and people carry them high.

They are paraded by the Government, newspapers, TV. Today's text speaks of God in action: 'he had made, He will carry.' In life, we may be easily led and lose the true God and real faith. We need to think better of it and return to our Lord Jesus Christ and His ways.

An eagle soaring in its pride over some valleys, covered with ice, saw a carcass lying exposed to view. The king of the birds came down and was so long feasting upon the carcass that when it wished to soar again, it was all in vain. The wings of the eagle had become frozen to the ice.

The world possesses influence which will chill and paralyse our souls if we do not take the greatest care.

Day Forty-Nine

Come unto me, all ye that labour and are heavy burdened, and I will give you rest.

St Matthew 11:28

To men and women today, brought face to face with conventional religion, comes the question 'Is this a thing I can carry?' or 'How much of it can I afford to carry?' this is an entirely false attitude. The question for today is surely the opposite. 'Can this faith carry me?' 'Can I afford to face life and the future without a Saviour?' The question of a creed does not enter into this. We have a living and lifting God awaiting our decision. No matter how great the worries and burdens; the loss of a job, of a near and dear one; ill health; a broken home, an unhappy marriage, the care of aged parents and relatives; an unsuccessful career; disappointing children; fear of the future, loneliness, temptation and sin – here is the answer, here is the Saviour tenderly pleading and whispering 'Come unto me'. In a city art gallery, there is a picture with the title *Into Thy hands*. A knight is shown mounted, journeying through a dense forest. He has reached a place of deepening darkness, gathering gloom and terrifying uncertainty. The faithful horse crouches in fear as if before the blow of an unseen antagonist. the rider himself sits erect and faces with serene confidence whatever trials and tortures the unseen path may hold. The hilt of his sword is in the shape of a cross and the secret of his composure is that mighty faith which, with the Cross as its symbol, can say, 'The way may be lost in darkness and dangers may attend with every step, but because thou will be with me, I will fear no evil – 'Into Thy Hands'.

God may not deliver us from the burning fiery furnace as He did not save the three men in Daniel's day, who were cast into a furnace heated seven times more than usual. Once we are in the fire then He will deliver us, which is an infinitely greater thing. 'And a fourth like unto the Son of God, will tread the flames with us.'

Day Fifty

> Bel boweth down, Nebo stoopeth... I carry, and will deliver you.
>
> Isaiah 46:1–4

Here the prophet strikes a note, who are Bel and Nebo? These are two idols. In the prophecy, it is still the eve of the capture of Babylon and he is picturing to himself what will happen on the morrow with the victory. The old-fashioned triumph will follow; the rifling of the temples; the carrying away of the defeated and discredited gods to be torn from their pedestals and trundled, head foremost, through the doors: 'Bel crouches, Nebo cowers'. The once proudly carried idols are now to become burdens themselves, slung over beasts' backs and packed off outside the city as useless dead weight.

Despite all this, God reveals Himself as a living and lifting God, ever constant in youth and old age, faithful from the cradle to the grave. A strong, unfailing Lord who carries, who saves. (See verses 3–7.)

When we step along, erect and quick, it is because we have a sense that assures the earth is firm, that gravitation will not fail, that our eyes, and the touch of our feet and our judgement of distance do not deceive us. If the body needs this, surely the soul needs a similar assurance. God alone can give this, so we may have faith and rise above circumstances, crises and trials. When the Holy Spirit is filling our lives, then we feel within us another self, purer, happier and victorious, inspired by the promises in the Word of God.

John Bunyan writes of the pilgrim climbing the Hill of Difficulty, who saw a lion on the right hand, and a lion on the left hand, and was too terrified to go on. At that moment, a cheering voice was heard from above, calling that the fierce lions were chained and need harm only those who approached the sides of the way.

> Every Joy or trial falleth from above, traced upon the dial by the Son of Love, we may trust Him fully, all for us to do, they who trust Him wholly find Him wholly true.

Day Fifty-One

'What sign shewest Thou unto us, seeing that Thou doest these things?' Jesus answered and said unto them, 'Destroy this temple, and in three days I will raise it up.' ...But he spake of the temple of His body.

St John 2:18–21

There is a graphic narrative in the Scriptures of our Lord Jesus Christ going first to the Temple on His visit to Jerusalem. There He found a veritable market. he did not complain to the priests, it would have been futile since they condoned the corruptions. Rather He took action to drive out the sheep and oxen with a scourge of small cords, their owners were sent following them. He threw the money changers' coins to the ground, He overturned the tables. Lastly, He said to the sellers of the doves, 'Take these things hence, make not my Father's house a house of merchandise.'

To honour God is to be blessed, to dishonour Him is to be condemned. We ask ourselves, 'What is the most grievous problem facing me, what is it that spoils our lives just now?'

Away in the battle line, a vital message came over the field telephone. 'We are going to advance, send reinforcements.' the poor empty-headed telephonist in the rear received the message, 'We are going to a dance, send three and fourpence.' Do we have the right interpretation of the things that matter most in life? We should make sure the Temple is pure, guided by the Scriptures and our inner selves. The Psalm writer stated, 'I will behold Thy face in righteousness, I shall be satisfied when I awake in Thy likeness.'

When we are filled with a love and passion for the Lord, it is then that all things fall into their proper perspective; those things which may be question-marked are settled for ever. Limitless possibilities are before believers. The Christian life is full of romance, circumstances are divinely revealed and controlled.

> Though all the changing scenes of life,
> In trouble and in joy,
> The praises of my God shall still
> My heart and tongue employ.

N. Tate and N. Brady
1696

Day Fifty-Two

Jesus saw a man named Matthew, sitting at the tax collector's booth. 'Follow me,' He told him and Matthew got up and followed Him.

St Matthew 9:9

Life is made up of decisions, which may vitally affect us for good or ill. We decide about our education, about our first job, changing the job, getting married, about a family and finally retiring and so on.

God expects us to pray and seek His guidance in our daily tasks – school, home, work and leisure – whether it is bench, desk, counter or sink. Sometimes, it is referred to as a 'calling', and there are instances in the Scriptures of people who our Lord Jesus Christ sought out; Peter, Andrew, James and John and also Matthew. He was not a fisherman but a tax collector. In a house by the lakeside he took the toll money from people who passed along the road or came over the lake, merchants with camels and asses, bearing bundles. He would inspect them as do Customs Officers today and prescribe a tax or charge. It was an unpopular task, especially as it was to be paid to the Romans; probably as a collector, Matthew would have been regarded as a traitor with his allegiance to the roman conquerors. More than this, the taxmen were often harsh and unfair, even to the extent of cheating the people. Today, people enjoy cheating the taxman! Maybe Matthew had thought about Jesus and His teachings. perhaps he had said to himself, 'I wonder if this Jesus will ever come my way and speak to me?' Jesus understands, He sees and knows us. One day, He came to Matthew, stopped, looked at him and spoke quietly to him, 'Follow me'. Matthew realised this was his big chance, the call of his life. Without hesitation he left everything and went with Christ and continued with him always. He wasn't seeking Him, but Jesus sought Matthew.

He never went back, indeed, he made a great feast and we know him as the one who wrote the Gospel according to St Matthew. The clear call of Christ still comes in the frantic busy world, sometimes not to leave but to stay where we are. He needs us very much in the place appointed, keeping the mundane things from becoming consuming and ambitious, and living as dedicated to Him.

Day Fifty-Three

> And this is my prayer; that your love may abound more in knowledge and in depth of insight, so that you may be able to discuss what is best and may be pure and blameless until the day of Christ.
>
> Philippians 1:9–10

In Australia, a big bridge collapsed, and many workmen were injured and killed. One man had a remarkable escape. 'Suddenly', he said, 'a huge gust of wind, created by the falling bridge, picked me up and carried me twenty yards through the air, this threw me clear and saved my life.'

Some would say this was 'miraculous', well, if they mean' unbelievable', 'wonderful', 'astonishing', who would object? If they say, 'it means God intervened to save his life', what then? Was this an answer to some prayer? Was he saved because he was an exceptionally good man? St Luke (13:4), records that our Lord Jesus Christ commented on a similar disaster in a place called Siloam, when a tower collapsed and eighteen were killed. Jesus asserted that it certainly did not follow that these eighteen victims were exceptionally wicked. Neither is it true that we get in this life what we deserve, good or bad. We realise this by experience and from what Jesus says. Are these 'Accidents', chance or bad luck? No, no, no, that is not the answer, there is no Lady Luck, or goddess of Fortune. The answer?

Science can explain what happened; the bridge collapsed due to faulty design, bad materials and poor workmanship.

Christian believers would say that God the Creator cares, as a Father in Heaven, for all His people upholding the whole order of nature. Is this done in an arbitrary way, or do we have a choice to make?

In the Old Testament, God is presented as revealing Himself in the history of Israel – His chosen people – as a parable of His saving love for them.

Yes, men and women do have a choice to make. In the New Testament our Lord Jesus Christ says, 'O Jerusalem, O Jerusalem, you who kill the prophets and stone those sent to you, how often I have longed to gather your children together, as a hen gathers her chicks under her wings, but you were not willing. Look, your house is left to you desolate.' (St Matthew 23:37.)

> I will sing the wondrous story
> Of the Christ who died for me

> F.H. Rowley
> 1886

Day Fifty-Four

Now therefore, give me this mountain...

Joshua 14:12

'Bless me and enlarge my coast, let your hand be with me and keep me from harm so that I will be free from pain,' and God granted his request.

1 Chronicles 4:10

Here we have, first Caleb, and in the second verse, Jabez, asking for a climbing and conquering faith in all their difficulties and dangers. What about the mountains or little hills in your life, are they getting you down, are you sliding downwards? have the giants, selfishness, discontent, greed, bad temper, uncontrollable tongue and so on, been driven out? Are you still unkind, inconsiderable, careless, indifferent, lazy? Are these giants ever going to be dislodged? Filled with the Holy Spirit of God, only then can we be blessed ourselves, and be a blessing to those around us. As a young man, Caleb was sent to spy out the land of Canaan; he showed faith by his unusual courage. the majority of the spies were dismayed and impressed by the difficulties to be overcome to possess the land. 'The people are strong... giants... the cities are fortified.'

Caleb stood up in faith against the crowd. He said, 'let us go up at once and occupy it, for we are well able to overcome it.' Later, in middle life, his faith gave him patience, he grew neither weary nor faint. Middle age can be a time of unrelenting pressures, frustration, a trap of unattainable dreams. Hard realities of life dawn upon us and breed cynicism. Forty years later, the Israelites were in the Promised Land, and Caleb, with a strength as strong as ever, despite his age, asked that he might be permitted to drive out the giants from the mountain stronghold (Joshua 15:14).

This spirit and courage, faith and faithfulness caused the giants to flee! In youth, middle and old age, God will lift us up, save us from falling away, becoming depressed, losing our first love or vision for His service. Jabez too, needed more land and, to help remove the enemy, the Canaanite, he prayed 'increase my vision – deepen my faith'.

Help us to be less parochial, take me further than the local scene, help me to see that, although in my own small world nothing much seems to be happening, God is mightily at work in His world.

There is the 'waters of trial' for diamonds; place the true and false stones under the water and there is a great difference. The imitation stone is practically submerged and the genuine shines out and sparkles. Both Caleb and Jabez were gems for God.

Day Fifty-Five

> And with great power gave the Apostles witness of the Resurrection of the Lord Jesus: and great grace was upon them all.
>
> Acts 4:33

It all depends on how we look at things! The few early disciples were no doubt regarded as a perfect nuisance but a short-lived 'nine days wonder', by the Roman state, the Jewish Church and many common people of those far-off days. On the other hand, they were laying the foundations of the early Christian Church. They were beginning to set forth the great challenge of the Lord Jesus Christ to the lives of men and women.

One time in the Dresden Art Gallery, there hung two famous paintings. Both were titled *The Head of Jesus Christ*. The one by Guido Reni was a tragic canvas of a pallid drooping blood-stained head, sweat stained face, crowned with a crown of thorns. A death stare in the eyes, and parched lips: the head of Jesus Christ. The second painting was by Caracci, but what a difference: a young man radiant in the golden sunlight, with strong, sensitive features, *lips* parted in a radiant smile, eyes aglow, brow adorned with flowing hair. A brave, tender winsome being. The most perfect and vital of all men, the Son of God.

This is the risen living Christ who saves men and women to live life with a capital 'L'; everlasting, eternal life, if they will accept Him. It all depends on how we look upon it. On the Cross, Jesus Christ is the Saviour of men and women. On the Cross Jesus Christ disturbs and damns men and women if they are outside Him. The challenge of Christ is still real today. In those early days, the Apostle asked, 'Was the Cross the end, was it to be utter abject defeat?' A few weeks later it was triumph, they were out in the streets aflame with a message; fearless, happy, full of great grace and conquering the earth. What brought the change? A living, risen Saviour.

Day Fifty-Six

Remember not, remember not the former things.
Behold I am doing a new thing, now it springs forth,
do you not perceive it?

Isaiah 43:18–19

We are often warned about the danger of the backward look. One epic illustration is that of the biblical story of Lot's wife. Plainly, her heart and whole life was in the city of Sodom. The sad day came when sinful Sodom was to be blasted from off the earth. It was a day for a complete uprooting and departure. The family of Lot left to escape the disaster, but his wife looked back and became a pillar of salt, caught up in the volcanic fall out and stopped dead in her tracks. A tragic end to what was to have been a new beginning. 'Remember not', is surprising, coming from Isaiah, as the prophet constantly says 'Remember'; remember the greatness and blessing of God to His people, remember His holy promise to bring forth His people with joy and His chosen with gladness, freeing them from later slavery in Egypt, to give them a land flowing with milk and honey'.

So often we suffer from nostalgia, looking back in our lives and particularly in our faith. Things were so real to us in those years gone by, but our faith may now be so limp and dead. To say that God to us was living then, is no comfort if He is dead now. God is the Lord of yesterday, today and tomorrow and for ever. This is the whole essence of our Christian living. 'Do you not perceive it?' 'Don't you see it?' Not because we are faithless, but because we are too faithful to the past, to the ways He dealt with us then, rather than to the new and exciting ways He proposes to open up to us now and in the future.

Day Fifty-Seven

'Come now, let us reason together,' saith the Lord: 'though your sins be as scarlet, they shall be as white as snow; though they be red like crimson, they shall be as wool.'

Isaiah 1:18

In all the swift patterns of life, we find new ways, strange ways, disturbing ways, pressing upon us. We may be so stuck in the trenches that we fear to leap up and out into the no man's land of God's way.

There are often conflicting issues and alternative ways of dealing with them. People try to help themselves and to find self-empowerment, to explore and negotiate one's own needs and be encouraged to make decisions. Each one of us must feel valued and willing to talk through and to explore the problem(s) openly: to increase the understanding of ourselves and consider what is open to us and choose the best course of action. Adjustment may have to be made to a situation that is unlikely to change, as with the terminally ill, then 'we whistle in the graveyard'.

Against this, there may be the possibility of progress, freedom and a great feeling of complete change and joy. Situations can be explored by being aware of the thoughts and issues, with a clear understanding of the problem, honestly, sincerely, without facades and pretensions. So with each problem be ready to take action, to weigh the cost, financially and physically.

Reasoning together will mean we consider discomforts, changes of lifestyle and possible side effects on family, work, leisure and spiritual demands. Seek help from firm friends. Always listen to others carefully, be warm, don't judge, be sincere and sensitive. Avoid manipulation, premature assessments and over-emotional states. Be consistent, without domination, be direct and trustworthy. Pray to know yourself. Remember *Pilgrim's Progress*:

> Just as Christian came up with the Cross, his burden loosed from his shoulders and fell from his back and began to tumble and so continued to do until it came to the mouth of the Sepulchre, where it fell in and I saw it no more.

Day Fifty-Eight

The Lord said, 'I have seen the misery of my people... the cry has reached me, so now go, I am sending you to Pharaoh to bring my people out of Egypt.'

Exodus 3:9–10

History shows that serious dangers are not always dramatic and not always seen to be disastrous. The greatest dangers are the insidious, quiet erosions of minds and hearts, peace, security, privilege and freedom.

When the extent of the erosion is realised it is too late, the irrevocable has happened, where it was once said, 'It cannot happen here'.

An illustration of this is the story of churches which, once thriving, are now redundant, demolished, closed or for sale and put to other uses; as museums, furniture warehouses, and countless other practices. The nation has let the Church decline and decay, its membership dwindling. Young people rarely darken the doors, except to leave quickly. Clergy and congregations become ever fewer and elderly, failing and discouraged. Christianity becomes unrecognisable and negligible by continual compromise to secularism and materialism. Is the Church of today to be quietly submerged, like a garden once beautiful, now covered by thick undergrowth, so that it has ceased to count, or will she shake herself free and bloom and blossom again? The solution is in God and His Son, the Lord Jesus Christ.

When Moses reached Midian, he found the same old story. Girls watering flocks were unjustly treated by selfish male shepherds. He acted and stood up for the things that mattered, and was received into their community. Years later came the transforming experience of his life, the unconsumed Burning Bush. There the presence and voice of God in reality came. As with Moses, so with us, it searches us out to act for Him in His ways, where every Christian has a committed part to play. Moses was chosen to bring them to the Land of Promise.

Day Fifty-Nine

For God, who commanded the light to shine out of darkness, hath shined in our hearts, to give the light of the knowledge of the glory of God in the face of Jesus Christ.

2 Corinthians 4:6

Years ago one of the Russian astronauts was quoted as saying he 'didn't see any God up there in space.' In contrast, a USA astronaut said, 'I didn't see God either, visually, but I saw some of the wonders He created. I felt as if God was no nearer to me and no further away than He always is, I need Him every day, in space and on earth. If you don't know Him down here, you won't find God one hundred and thirty miles high up there. We all should seek Him and accept Him into our hearts, I don't feel that a person can ever really be at peace otherwise.'

Many people live in fear – of old age and death, sickness accident, poverty, unemployment, family, fear of losing friends and relatives; fear of loneliness, of the phone ringing and bringing bad news, and so on. The antidote, the answer, lies in God.

Jesus once spoke of a merchant who spent his time and money and every effort collecting precious pearls. Then he came to the pearl above all pearls, and he gave up the rest and took a firm hold of the pearl of great price. This is Jesus himself, our Lord and Saviour. We may have many precious pearls, art, science, philosophy, good living, excellent integrity, morals above reproach, even good religion, but we need, above all else, to lay hold of the unique and matchless jewel – Jesus, in simple belief and trust.

Day Sixty

> The man believed what Jesus had said and started for home... while he was still on the way, his servants met him with the news that his boy was living. His father realised that this was the exact time at which Jesus said to him, 'Your son will live.'
>
> St John 4:50–53

Have you ever thought of the influence of Christ? It is all-reaching. Each age or stage of development through nearly the last two thousand years, in human culture or activity, has felt the incalculable direct effects. The indirect effects, which often people refuse to acknowledge, are wider still. This universal and irresistible influence has changed men and women and their ways – the hardest of all to do – bringing benefits and regeneration with a deeper, richer satisfaction than anything else the world can experience.

He meets its lawlessness by announcing His sovereignty over it: 'I have overcome the world.' He meets its need of salvation by giving Himself, His life for it. He meets its need of hope by His promises for the future and His return to reign over it. He does not judge or condemn it, neither does He condone it, 'The world hateth me because I testify of it, that the works thereof are evil.' (St John 7:7) It is He who daily meets our needs, He who calls us to live out our Christianity in our own sphere of life, 'you in your small corner and I in mine'.

There is the vivid story of the nobleman, whose son is desperately ill – to the very point of death. He hears about Jesus and seeks Him out to beg Him to come and cure his son. He pleads, 'Sir, come down before my son dies.' Jesus tells him to return home with the assurance that his son will live. The man obeys; He believes in Jesus, in what He says and has promised. He goes home to be met by his servants with the joyful news that his son is going to live. They tell him the exact time at which the fever subsided and he began to mend, the same time as when he pleaded with the Saviour.

Here is faith, called for and described, aroused and exercised, Jesus ready to heal and make whole and restore for one who comes with real desire. The end? 'He and all his household became believers.'

Day Sixty-One

[Jesus said,] 'walk while ye have the light, lest darkness come upon you: for he that walketh in darkness knoweth not whither he goeth.'

St John 12:35

Only when we experience an awful blackout do we realise, as never before, the true value of light. Spiritual darkness of ourselves brings to us our great need of Christ, the true light. 'While ye have the light, believe in the light, that ye may be children of light.' 'More light' has been the human cry down the ages. Where are we? What are we? Whence are we? Where are we going? What is there above and beyond this world?

The answers are in our Lord Jesus Christ, to refuse His revelations is our condemnation.

A Christian lady was travelling with her husband, her attention was drawn to a fellow passenger, a young lady obviously in feeble health, not only in body but despondent and wretched in mind. Talking to her, the lady with great tact directed the sick girl to spiritual things. Presently, the tears began to flow as she said, 'I have never had anyone to show such interest in me before. I have been a gay, reckless and thoughtless creature and am fast drawing near the grave. I am in great darkness, can you show me light?'

Then her travelling companion told her of Him, who is the light of the world. When the train reached the station where the two must part, the sick girl clasped her newly found friend in one long, fervent embrace saying, 'God assuredly sent you to me, I can and do trust my Saviour now, we shall meet no more in this world, but I shall pray that I may meet you in the better world hereafter.'

God's light is life-giving, we feel the joy of life on the hills and in the valleys, where the sun is smiling and the wind waves the ripening corn.

List of Citations

Day One	Philippians 4:11–12
Day Two	Ecclesiastes 1:7
Day Three	Jeremiah 50:5
Day Four	Acts 26:28
Day Five	St Matthew 26:11
Day Six	St John 3:7–9
Day Seven	Joel 2:13
Day Eight	Genesis 21:6
Day Nine	Isaiah 28:21
Day Ten	Daniel 5:27–31
Day Eleven	2 Chronicles 26:5–16
Day Twelve	Isaiah 6:1
Day Thirteen	Isaiah 6:8
Day Fourteen	2 Timothy 2:15
Day Fifteen	Genesis 3:8–9
Day Sixteen	1 John 2:8
Day Seventeen	Judges 13:8

Day Eighteen	Psalm 39:1
Day Nineteen	1 Samuel 6:13–21
Day Twenty	Job 22:21
Day Twenty-One	Genesis 8:13–18
Day Twenty-Two	1 Samuel 2:18–19
Day Twenty-Three	St John 2:5
Day Twenty-Four	Romans 16:1–2
Day Twenty-Five	Zechariah 3:3
Day Twenty-Six	1 Peter 5:8–9
Day Twenty-Seven	St Luke 21:28
Day Twenty-Eight	Romans 13:11–12
Day Twenty-Nine	Romans 8:20–21
Day Thirty	St John 19:27
Day Thirty-One	St Mark 4:34
Day Thirty-Two	1 John 2:15
Day Thirty-Three	St Matthew 6:33–34
Day Thirty-Four	Jeremiah 10:23
Day Thirty-Five	St Mark 9:41
Day Thirty-Six	St Mark 11:22
Day Thirty-Seven	Genesis 24:27
Day Thirty-Eight	Psalm 23:1–2

Day Thirty-Nine	Numbers 21:4
Day Forty	Ephesians 2:4–5
Day Forty-One	St Luke 11:1
Day Forty-Two	1 Thessalonians 5:17
Day Forty-Three	St Matthew 21:22
Day Forty-Four	St John 6:68–69
Day Forty-Five	St Matthew 16:15
Day Forty-Six	St Mark 7:37
Day Forty-Seven	Colossians 1:23
Day Forty-Eight	Isaiah 46:4
Day Forty-Nine	St Matthew 11:28
Day Fifty	Isaiah 46:1–4
Day Fifty-One	St John 2:18–21
Day Fifty-Two	St Matthew 9:9
Day Fifty-Three	Philippians 1:9–10
Day Fifty-Four	1 Chronicles 4:10
Day Fifty-Five	Acts 4:33
Day Fifty-Six	Isaiah 43:18–19
Day Fifty-Seven	Isaiah 1:18
Day Fifty-Eight	Exodus 3:9–10
Day Fifty-Nine	2 Corinthians 4:6

Day Sixty   St John 4:50–53

Day Sixty-One   St John 12:35